The City

LIFE IN ELIZABETHAN ENGLAND

The City

KATHRYN HINDS

MARSHALL CAVENDISH BENCHMARK NEW YORK

To the wonderful teachers of Lumpkin County High School

The author and publisher specially wish to thank Dr. Megan Lynn Isaac,
former associate professor of Renaissance Literature at Youngstown State University, Ohio,
for her invaluable help in reviewing the manuscript.

MARSHALL CAVENDISH BENCHMARK 99 WHITE PLAINS ROAD TARRYTOWN, NEW YORK 10591-9001
www.marshallcavendish.us Text copyright © 2008 by Marshall Cavendish Corporation All rights reserved. No part of
this book may be reproduced or utilized in any form or by any means electronic or mechanical including photocopying,
recording, or by any information storage and retrieval system, without permission from the copyright holders. All
Internet sites were available and accurate when this book was sent to press. Library of Congress Cataloging-in-
Publication Data Hinds, Kathryn, 1962- The City / by Kathryn Hinds. p. cm. — (Life in Elizabethan England)
Summary: "A social history of Elizabethan England, focusing on life among the merchants, craftspeople, and other city
dwellers during the reign (1558-1603) of the famous monarch"—Provided by publisher. Includes bibliographical references and index. ISBN 978-0-7614-2544-1 1. England—Social life and customs—16th century—Juvenile literature.
2. Cities and towns—England—History—16th century—Juvenile literature. 3. Great Britain—History—Elizabeth,
1558-1603—Juvenile literature. I. Title. II. Series. DA355.H557 2007   942.05'5—dc22   2007006385

EDITOR: Joyce Stanton   PUBLISHER: Michelle Bisson
ART DIRECTOR: Anahid Hamparian   SERIES DESIGNER: Michael Nelson

Printed in Malaysia
135642

front cover: A newly married couple leave a London church in this Elizabethan scene imagined by nineteenth-century artist
Edmund Blair Leighton.
half-title page: A little boy feeds berries to his pet bird. He posed for this portrait in 1572.
title page: Friends gather around a new mother to celebrate the birth of her child.
back cover: Famed Elizabethan jeweler and artist Nicholas Hilliard painted this miniature portrait of his wife, Alice, in 1578.

CONTENTS

A husband and wife in 1592, their elegant clothes accented
with lace cuffs and lace-trimmed ruffs

About Elizabethan England

IT WAS A GOLDEN AGE: A TIME OF POETRY, THEATER, AND SONG; intrigue, adventure, and exploration; faith, intellect, and passion; trials, triumphs, and splendor. The reign of Elizabeth I, from 1558 to 1603, was like no other era of English history. Under Elizabeth's leadership, England began the journey from small, isolated, poor island nation to thriving world power. Under the poets and playwrights of Elizabeth's time—above all, William Shakespeare—the English language reached new heights, and a powerful body of literature was created, one that still delights and inspires us. Elizabeth invited and influenced other forms of creativity as well, and her rule left indelible marks not only in the arts but in politics, religion, and society. The glories—and the troubles—of her reign are all part of the heritage shared by England and its former colonies.

This series of books looks at the Elizabethan age with a focus on its people and their everyday lives, whether they were at the top of society, the bottom, or somewhere in the middle. We will see how they worked, where they lived, how they related to one another, how they relaxed and celebrated special occasions, how they coped with life's hardships. In this volume we will meet the people of Elizabethan England's cities: merchants and mayors, tradeswomen and housewives, actors and students, and more. These people had many of the same joys and sorrows, hopes and fears that we do. They were poised at the beginning of the modern age, but still their world was very different from ours. Forget about telephones, computers, cars, and televisions, and step back in time. . . . Welcome to life in Elizabethan England!

London

But now behold,
In the quick forge and working-house of thought,
How London doth pour out her citizens.
— SHAKESPEARE, *HENRY V*

IN THE SIXTEENTH CENTURY, ENGLAND WAS A MAINLY rural nation; towns of more than five thousand were home to just 8 percent of the population. Many towns had only a few streets, with gardens and orchards among the shops and houses. Farm animals were a common sight—most people raised some chickens and pigs, and the well-off had horses (if you couldn't afford a horse, you had to walk everywhere). Some townspeople even worked at farming, at least part-time—nearly all cities were surrounded by farm fields. Links between country and city were strong, with city people exchanging their goods and services for the agricultural products of country people. Sometimes business was handled by middlemen, but often farmers and townspeople made their transactions face to face at urban fairs and markets.

Opposite: London was an ancient city even in Elizabeth's time, when a section of its Roman wall was still standing.

9

ENGLAND'S CAPITAL

During Elizabeth's reign, more and more people moved from the countryside to urban areas. London's population went from roughly 120,000 in 1550 to around 200,000 in 1600, becoming the third largest city in Europe (only Paris and Naples were bigger). The other major English cities were Norwich, Bristol, Newcastle, and York, each of which had between 10,000 and 30,000 residents in 1600. But when people spoke of "going to town," it was always London that they meant.

Elizabeth's London was made up of two main sections, Westminster and the City of London. The City was an area of about one square mile, bounded by the Thames River on the south and enclosed the rest of the way around by a high wall originally built by the ancient Romans. Westminster lay just to the west, connected to the City by a road called the Strand, along which many nobles had mansions with gardens that ran right down to the bank of the river. The Thames was really London's main highway, and people

did much of their traveling by barge and ferry and other boats. There was only one bridge across, linking the City to growing suburbs on the south bank.

London was England's major city in every way. First, it was the capital, the center of government. In and around the city were Queen Elizabeth's principal palaces, where she received ambassadors, gave audiences, made decisions, and conferred with the members of her Privy Council (an advisory and administrative group, similar to the president's Cabinet). Westminster was home to Whitehall Palace, the Court of Justice, and the meeting place of Parliament. German traveler Paul Hentzner visited all these places in 1598, recording interesting details about them in his diary; for example: "In the chamber where the Parliament is usually held, the seats and wainscot are made of wood, the growth of Ireland; said to have that occult [mysterious] quality, that all poisonous animals are driven away by it."

The presence of the royal court made London the cultural cen-

London viewed from the south bank of the Thames. On the lower left, the four circular buildings with flags flying are theaters. The big church across the river is the old Saint Paul's Cathedral, which burned down in 1666. London Bridge links the two riverbanks. Atop the bridge's gatehouse, traitors' heads are displayed on pikes.

A busy printer's shop around 1600. On the left, compositors select type from cases in front of them. Toward the back of the shop, a worker coats the set type with ink. In front of him, another worker operates the printing press, screwing the plate of set and inked type down onto a sheet of paper. On the far right, the master printer, owner of the shop, supervises.

ter of England, since the queen and courtiers were passionately fond of music, dancing, poetry, and plays. Some of the finest composers and musicians in Europe lived and worked in London. From time to time, average Londoners had the opportunity to hear court music at public celebrations. And much of the same music enjoyed by the English nobility was published by London printers, so that well-off people could buy it to play or sing at home.

Poetry, too, could be found both at court and at the booksellers'. Quite a few members of the court wrote poetry, most notably Sir Philip Sidney. Handwritten books of poems were often passed around among groups of friends—this was how Sidney's poems, for example, were first distributed. But more and more writers were having their works printed. London, with about two dozen printing presses by the 1580s, was the hub of the English publishing industry—in fact, books could be legally printed only in London and the two university towns, Oxford and Cambridge.

The printers published all kinds of works: religious writings, ancient Greek and Roman literature, textbooks, cookbooks, and much, much more. One kind of publication, though, was becoming increasingly popular: drama. The Elizabethans were some of the most enthusiastic playgoers of all time, and many were discovering that they enjoyed reading plays almost as much as seeing them on the stage. There were a number of playwrights working in London during Elizabeth's reign, but the greatest were Christopher Marlowe, William Shakespeare, and Ben Jonson (all three wrote nondramatic poetry, too). Shakespeare was also a leading member of the famed acting company known as the Lord Chamberlain's Men, who owned their own theater, the Globe (built in 1599). London was the only place in England that had permanent playhouses; elsewhere actors had to perform in inns or private homes.

London, especially the City, dominated in business and commerce as in everything else. As an island nation, England did a great deal of trade by shipping, sending out exports and bringing in imports from near and far. In his 1587 *Description of England*, William Harrison painted this picture of England's active merchant fleet:

> The wares that they carry out of the realm are for the most part broadcloths and carfies [prepared cloth] of all colours, likewise cottons, friezes [coarse woollen cloth], rugs, tin, wool, lead, fells [hides], etc; which being shipped at sundry ports of our coasts are borne from thence into all quarters of the world, and there either exchanged for other wares or ready money, to the great gain and commodity of our merchants. And whereas in times past their chief trade was into Spain, Portugal, France, Flanders [modern Belgium], Dansk [Denmark], Norway, Scotland and Iceland only, now in these days, as men not contented with these journeys, they have sought out the East and West Indies, and made voyages not

THE Silkewormes, and their Flies:

Liuely deſcribed in verſe, by T. M. a *Countrie Farmar*, and an apprentice in Phyſicke.

For the great benefit and enriching of England.

Printed at London by V. S. for Nicholas Ling, and are to be ſold at his ſhop at the Weſt ende of Paules. 1599.

The title page of a 1599 book about raising silkworms, "lively described in verse." It was both printed and sold in a shop near Saint Paul's Cathedral. The neighborhood around Saint Paul's was the center of England's publishing and bookselling industry.

only unto the Canaries and New Spain, but likewise into Cathay [China], Moscovia [Russia], . . . and the regions thereabout, from whence, as they say, they bring home great commodities.

England had a number of port cities—Plymouth, Bristol, Exeter, and others—where merchandise could be shipped in and out, but much of this commercial activity was run from London, and the bulk of the goods and profits ended up there. For that matter, London itself had plenty of shipyards and docks, so that Swiss traveler Thomas Platter remarked, "Ocean-craft are accustomed to run in here in great numbers as into a safe harbour, and I myself beheld one large galley next the other . . . , some hundred vessels in all, nor did I ever behold so many large ships in one port in my life."

As England became more powerful and self-confident on the seas, business boomed. During Elizabeth's lifetime, London investors founded several companies focused on international trade, including the Muscovy Company (with a monopoly on trade to Russia), the Eastland Company (which controlled English trade in Scandinavia and the Baltic countries), the Levant Company (trading primarily with Turkey), and the East India Company. Established in 1600, the East India Company would eventually become so powerful and influential that it would rule India.

RUNNING THE CITY

The City of London had had its own elected government since 1215. It was headed by the Lord Mayor. He held office for only one year, but his authority in the City was immense, and only the queen or the Privy Council could overrule his decisions. After he was elected, the Lord Mayor stepped into his official barge and was rowed up the Thames to Westminster to swear his loyalty to the queen. His barge was accompanied by those belonging to the City's livery companies, influential organizations of craftspeople and tradespeople. It was a great spectacle—banners and streamers flying, coats of arms on display, trumpets playing and cannon firing—that set the tone for his whole year in office. Paul Hentzner was quite impressed with the Lord Mayor and the pageantry surrounding him:

The Lord Mayor of London, in his scarlet robe and gold chain of office, confers with an alderman *(center)* and a representative of one of the city's livery companies.

> During the year of his magistracy, he is obliged to live so magnificently, that foreigner or native, without any expense, is free, if he can find a chair empty, to dine at his table, where there is always the greatest plenty. When the mayor goes out of the precincts of the city, a sceptre, a sword, and a cap, are borne before him, and he is followed

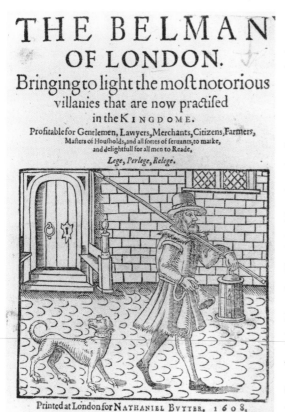

THE BELMAN
OF LONDON.

Bringing to light the moſt notorious
villanies that are now practiſed
in the KINGDOME.

Profitable for Gentlemen, Lawyers, Merchants, Citizens, Farmers,
Maſters of Houſholds, and all ſortes of ſeruants, to marke,
and delightfull for all men to Reade.

Lege, Perlege, Relege.

Printed at London for NATHANIEL BVTTER. 1608.

by the principal aldermen in scarlet gowns, with gold chains; himself and they on horseback.

There were twenty-four aldermen in all. They were high-ranking members of the livery companies, which elected them. Each alderman represented a different ward, or region, of the City, which he also served as justice of the peace. As a group, the aldermen were in charge of the City's finances and other affairs, and it was their duty to see the queen's and Privy Council's orders followed in their wards. Every year the aldermen selected one of their number to be Lord Mayor of London. They also elected two men to serve one-year terms as sheriffs of London. The sheriffs assisted the Lord Mayor in such matters as collecting taxes, overseeing the criminal courts, and presenting the City's needs to Parliament.

To take care of many administrative matters and supervise various officials, alderman had assistants, such as the constables and watchmen who were charged with keeping the peace. Carrying staffs and lanterns, the watchmen patrolled their wards at night, on the lookout for thieves, disorderly drunks, fires getting out of control, and other types of trouble—at least, they were supposed to. But in *Much Ado about Nothing*, Shakespeare portrayed a constable and watchmen who don't exactly inspire confidence. When the constable orders the watchmen to "make no noise in the streets," one of them answers, "We will rather sleep than talk. We know what

Watchmen were also called bell-men, because each carried a bell that he would ring to alert the neighborhood in case of trouble.

belongs to a watch." The constable's response to this is, "Why, you speak like an ancient and most quiet watchman, for I cannot see how sleeping should offend." Elizabethan playgoers laughing at this comic scene may well have been reminded of inefficient or bumbling officials from the wards they lived in.

Although London had its own government, many English cities of this time period did not. Only a city with a royal charter could govern itself. A charter granted the city the right to elect not only local officials but also two men to represent it in Parliament. In addition a chartered, or incorporated, city could collect taxes, tolls, fines, rents, and profits from fairs and markets. In a city without a charter, these financial advantages, along with governmental control, belonged to the national government or to the nobleman who owned the land on which the city was built. Not surprisingly, a number of cities sought charters, even though they had to purchase the privilege from the crown. Elizabeth granted charters of incorporation to thirty-two cities during the course of her reign, adding sixty-four new members to Parliament's House of Commons.

City Scenes

*The greatest part of our building in the cities and good towns of England
consisteth only of timber, for as yet few of the houses
of the commonality . . . are made of stone.*
— WILLIAM HARRISON, *THE DESCRIPTION OF ENGLAND*, 1587

IMAGINE YOU ARE COMING TO VISIT AN ENGLISH CITY during Elizabeth's time. The road you're traveling is unpaved, full of ruts and potholes. The traffic is mostly people on foot or horseback, and carts carrying various goods to the city. You may see a few wealthy people riding in carriages, but these are slow and uncomfortable. You pass through country villages and among fields, pastures, and hedgerows. Then you see the city walls. They are old, dating back to the Middle Ages or even to the days when Britain was part of the Roman Empire. Some cities don't have walls, but a city without a wall is likely to be surrounded by some other kind of barrier, such as a ditch. In any case, to enter the city, you have to pass through a gateway, where you probably have to pay a toll. The gatehouse, since it's always guarded, may double as a jail. But you don't have to worry about that; after paying your toll, and maybe answering some questions about your business, you're free to explore the city.

Opposite: This tall, fine house was the London residence of a French nobleman sent as an ambassador to Elizabeth's court.

19

An inn scene by a twentieth-century artist illustrates a situation described by Elizabethan writers: sometimes an innkeeper gave information about a guest's travel plans to a highwayman, who would then rob the guest on the road and share the money with the crooked innkeeper.

PUBLIC PLACES

Before seeing the sights, you would probably want to check into an inn. William Harrison's *Description of England* sums up English inns this way:

> Such is the capacity of some of them that they are able to lodge two hundred or three hundred persons and their horses at least, and thereto with a very short warning make such provision for their diet, as to him that is unacquainted withal may seem to be incredible. Howbeit of all in England there are no worse inns than in London, and yet many are there far better than the best I have heard of in any foreign country.

Your inn is likely to be near a market, one of the first places you might visit. It will probably be a large open area at a crossroads or a place where a main street widens out. In many towns the marketplace is designated by a large stone cross, known as a market cross. Some cities have covered marketplaces, or even large market halls.

Whether the market is indoors or outdoors, it will have booths and stalls where merchants, craftspeople, and farmers sell all kinds of goods, foodstuffs, and livestock. And many cities have a number of specialized markets. In Leicester, for example, you would find separate marketing areas for hay and grain, wood, sheep, horses, and meat.

Markets were overseen by city officials who checked quality, set prices, and made sure that weights and measures were accurate (since many things were sold by weight). In smaller towns there might be only one or two market days a week, but in London the markets were open every day except Sunday—sellers from outside the city, however, might only be permitted to do business on Wednesdays and Saturdays. London markets dealt mainly in such commodities as meat, fish, poultry, dairy products, vegetables, and fruit. Some food items could also be bought from street vendors, bakeries, or grocery shops.

Cities had shops that sold all kinds of crafted and manufactured goods—everything from gloves to books to ironwork. People in the same craft or trade tended to have their shops on the same street or in the same neighborhood; Paul Hentzner remarked in particular on the goldsmiths' street in London:

> The streets in this city are very handsome and clean; but that which is named from the goldsmiths who inhabit it, surpasses all the rest; there is in it a gilt tower, with a fountain that plays. Near it, on the farther side, is a handsome house built by a goldsmith and presented by him to the city. There are besides to be seen in this street, as in all others where there are goldsmiths' shops, all sorts of gold and silver vessels exposed to sale . . . in such quantities as must surprise a man the first time he sees and considers them.

A Farewell to London

Isabella Whitney was one of the few Elizabethan women writers whose work made it into print—she may in fact have been the first Englishwoman to have nonreligious poetry published. The following selections are from her poem "Will and Testament"; in it, she imagines that she has to leave London and so bequeaths to the city various legacies, giving us a lively picture of the city's neighborhoods, trades, and people.

Watling Street and Canwick Street
  I full of woolen leave,
And linen store in Friday Street,
  if they me not deceive.
And those which are of calling such
  that costlier they require,
I mercers leave, with silk so rich
  as any would desire.
In Cheap,* of them they store shall find,
  and likewise in that street
I goldsmiths leave, with jewels such
  as are for ladies meet. . . .

To all the bookbinders by Paul's,
  because I like their art,
They every week shall money have
  when they from books depart.**
Amongst them all my printer must
  have somewhat to his share;
I will my friends these books to buy
  of him, with other ware.
For maidens poor, I widowers rich
  do leave, that oft shall dote
And by that means shall marry them,
  to set the girls afloat.
And wealthy widows will I leave
  to help young gentlemen,
Which when you have, in any case
  be courteous to them then. . . .

*Cheapside, a main street and market center, which had many goldsmiths and dealers in fine fabrics

**when they sell their books

Street vendors selling chickens *(bottom)* and combs, eyeglasses, and other accessories *(top)*

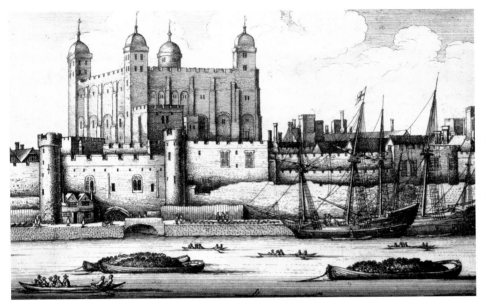

The Tower of London was and still is one of London's most popular tourist attractions. It was a royal fortress, but once Elizabeth became queen, the only time she stayed there was right before her coronation ceremony, as custom required.

Hentzner also described the Royal Exchange, a kind of Elizabethan shopping mall where both English and foreign merchants sold hats, clothes, wigs, accessories, perfumes, and similar goods, many of them imported: "It has a great effect, whether you consider the stateliness of the building, the assemblage of different nations, or the quantities of merchandise."

With your business completed in the shops and markets, what other places might you visit in an Elizabethan city? London, of course, had many attractions. Tourists often made a point of going to the theaters and the arenas where animal fights were held. They also wanted to see famous historic sites. There was Westminster Abbey, the great church where many English monarchs and nobles were entombed. The Tower of London had displays of armor and tapestries and royal jewels, not to mention a menagerie where lions lived. It was a notorious prison, too, in which powerful courtiers might be confined—and sometimes executed. As a young princess, Elizabeth herself had been held there for a time, under suspicion of plotting against her half sister, Queen Mary.

Elizabeth's palaces in and near the city offered tours of the royal rooms when she was not in residence. The *Golden Hind*, the ship in which Sir Francis Drake made his three-year around-the-world voyage (1577–1580), was a very popular attraction at its moorings just outside London. Many people loved to watch the hundreds of beautiful swans swimming in the Thames River. And London Bridge—"a bridge of stone eight hundred feet in length, of wonderful work"—was a sight you could hardly miss, "covered on each side with houses so disposed as to have

London Bridge was so crowded with houses, shops, horses, and carts that it could take as long as an hour to get from one end to the other. Pedestrians in a hurry usually crossed the river in small boats called wherries, which we might think of as water taxis.

the appearance of a continued street, not at all of a bridge." It had a gruesome aspect, however: "Upon this is built a tower, on whose top the heads of such as have been executed for high treason are placed on iron spikes: we counted above thirty," wrote Paul Hentzner.

A number of towns, especially in Wales, were dominated by medieval castles, usually built on the highest ground. But castles, though impressive, were rarely of any importance in the peaceful England and Wales of Elizabeth's time. Churches, however, whether built during the Middle Ages or more recently, had a prominent place in city life and ranged from small neighborhood churches to huge, magnificent cathedrals. In most towns, churches were the main public buildings. A city with the right of self-government, however, might have a town hall, which would be a great source of pride to the citizens (London's, built in 1411, was called Guildhall and is still standing). Both churches and town halls could house meetings, schools, law courts, and musters of the local militia—they were much more multipurpose than similar buildings today.

HOME SWEET HOME

For a great many city people, their place of business was also their home. Even wealthy investors, rich merchants, and government officials had home offices where they did a lot of their work. In a craftsman's or tradesman's house, all or most of the ground floor was work space. If there was a shop, it would be at the front, where there might be a big window to display the products for sale. The shutter of this window often opened downward to form a counter outside the shop; it would have an awning over it to protect it from the weather.

This twentieth-century illustration shows a cutaway view of the inside of a shoemaker's house, with his shop on the ground floor and living quarters above. Customers gather in the street, where a water bearer calls out that he has water for sale.

Most people's homes were very crowded, and there was little privacy. In the average household, parents and children shared the same bedroom. And many houses were home to other people besides the family. Anyone who could afford to have servants had at least one or two; the wealthy, of course, had many more. In a large house, servants could have their own quarters, but in smaller dwellings the servants might sleep in their master's room. Craftspeople often had apprentices living in their homes, and many families earned extra income by renting out rooms. At mealtimes, everyone—family members, servants, apprentices, boarders—gathered around the same table to eat together; only in the wealthiest households did servants have a separate place to eat.

Paul Hentzner made these observations about the homes of the English: "Their houses are commonly of two storeys, except in London, where they are of three and four, though but seldom of four; they are built of wood, those of the richer sort with bricks, their roofs are low, and, where the owner has money, covered with lead." Where the owner had less money, the roof was clay tiles, plain wooden shingles, or thatch. Another detail not mentioned by Hentzner is that the upper floors of many city houses jutted out over the street. Rows of one- or two-storied cottages were also found in Elizabethan towns—urban landowners were building more and more of these as "tenements," or houses to be rented out.

Row cottages and other small city houses had only one or two rooms on a floor. The residences of successful craftsmen and tradesmen, on the other hand, could include not just the family home but other buildings, such as workshops and warehouses, all arranged around a yard. Less prosperous home owners might share a yard with their neighbors. There could be a well and an outhouse in the yard, and room to hang out laundry, grow some vegetables, and keep a few chickens or maybe a pig.

WATER AND WASTE People who had no access to a well got their water from a public fountain or from water carriers who sold water door to door; the water could be stored in barrels to be used as needed. Nearly all towns were built by a river, which was usually the source of the water piped to fountains and sold by the watermen; many city dwellers fetched water themselves from the river or its conduits. Some wealthy people had water piped right into their homes. River water wasn't very clean, though, because sewage and other kinds of waste were routinely dumped into it.

Trash disposal was a problem. In London each ward had officials

On one end of London Bridge, wheels turned by the current powered pumps that raised water from the river. These waterworks, however, supplied only a portion of the growing city's needs.

called scavengers who were supposed to make sure the streets stayed clean, but it's hard to know how they did it. Some kinds of garbage would be fed to pigs or would be eaten by dogs and other animals. Kitchen waste could often be recycled—fireplace ashes and animal fat were used to make soap, and vegetable matter could be turned into compost to enrich garden soil. On the whole, people threw away a lot less than most Americans do today and recycled as much as possible. For example, there were many shops that sold used clothes. And ragmen bought worn-out clothing and cloth scraps, which they could resell to papermakers.

People tried to stay as clean as they could. Because it was so difficult to get and heat a large amount of water, most rarely took a bath, but they used a washbasin and jug to cleanse their hands and face every morning. They also washed hands before each meal and after going to the bathroom. If they didn't have an outhouse in the yard or an indoor latrine (often called a jakes), they could use a chamber pot or a closestool (basically a box with a hole in the top and a chamber pot inside; wealthy people's closestools had padded seats). Instead of toilet paper, small pieces of cloth were used—and they were washed out and reused many times.

THE COMFORTS OF HOME The insides of houses naturally varied according to the owners' wealth. Poor people's homes were dark and plain. To conserve heat, there were just a few, small windows, and they might not even have glass in them. The average house had only one heat source, either a fireplace or an open hearth—this was also where cooking was done. Wood was the usual fuel, but coal mining became an important industry during Elizabeth's reign. The coal was used largely in manufacturing (in the kilns of glassmakers and brickmakers, for example), but poorer city dwellers in some parts of the country were beginning to cook and heat their homes with coal. It produced a sooty smoke, though, which added to the discomforts people lived with.

The homes of the well-to-do were brighter and warmer, with many large windows, and fireplaces in every room. Wall hangings—either tapestries or painted cloths—added insulation as well as decoration. Artificial light came from fine beeswax candles (the less well-off had tallow candles, oil lamps, or rushes dipped in grease—called rushlights—all of which could use animal fat left over from cooking). Sixteenth-century candles worked differently from the ones we have today: to keep them burning strong and bright, you had to carefully trim the wick about every half hour. Among the luxuries wealthy people enjoyed were candlesticks made of silver; candlesticks were also available in less expensive materials, such as brass and clay.

Elizabethan homes were not crowded with furniture. The hall, or main room, would contain a rectangular dining table. People sat around it on either stools or benches. Many families owned only one chair, which was for the head of the family. Of course, wealthy families could have several chairs, and cushions to pad them. Most chairs had arms, except for farthingale chairs. These were made to

accommodate fashionable women's huge skirts, which were supported by cylindrical or bell-shaped structures of wood, whalebone, or wire called farthingales. The other main piece of furniture in the hall would be a chest or cupboard to store plates, platters, cups, spoons, tablecloths, and so on. In smaller homes, the hall was also the kitchen, so it would have everything needed for storing and cooking food as well as for serving and eating it. Very few kitchens, however, had ovens—bread had to be purchased from the neighborhood bakery.

Some city houses were so small that there was only one room. The family would have to sleep as well as work, cook, and eat there. Most houses, though, had at least one separate bedroom, usually on an upper floor. This room's main piece of furniture was, of course, the bed. Like most other furniture, the bed frame would be made of English oak. Beds could be very big, although few were as large as the Great Bed at the White Hart Inn in the town of Ware, which had room for at least seven people! (Built in 1590, this bed was a tourist attraction, so famous that Shakespeare even men-

The Great Chamber of a house once owned by Elizabeth's father, Henry VIII. Elizabeth gave it to her cousin, the poet and playwright (and later her Lord Treasurer) Thomas Sackville. The furniture here is from a slightly later period, but the fireplace and the plasterwork on the ceiling and walls are from the 1500s to early 1600s.

The Great Bed of Ware, now on exhibit in the Victoria and Albert Museum in London. In Elizabethan times it would have had not only a mattress and bolsters, but heavy curtains hanging around it.

tioned it in his play *Twelfth Night*: "although the sheet were big enough for the bed of Ware.")

Beds were surrounded with curtains to help keep sleepers warm and give them a little more privacy. Wealthy people's bed curtains were of sumptuous fabrics or heavily embroidered and were among their proudest possessions. Quilts and coverlets could be equally rich; blankets were of wool, and sheets of linen; mattresses and pillows were stuffed with goose or swan feathers—or straw and similar materials for poorer people. The bedroom might also contain chests for storing clothes and bed linens, a mirror, a cradle if there was a baby in the family, and a trundle bed (pulled out from under the big bed) for older children or servants to sleep in.

During the fifteenth century, homes for the middle and upper classes grew larger, with more rooms. This was the time period when rooms began to develop specialized purposes. For example, many houses now had a parlor, intended for leisure-time activities with family and friends, such as playing games, playing and listening to music, and reading aloud together. Another special room was the head of the family's study, where he kept his books and papers. But as houses began to be divided up into areas for specific activities, the idea grew that certain family members belonged more in some parts of the house than others. Children might be expected to stay in the nursery rooms, while the wife might spend most of her time in the kitchen area and a small private chamber, near the bedroom, referred to as her closet. The father of the family, however, continued to have the run of the whole house.

Men at Work

Are not these my brave men, brave shoemakers,
all gentlemen of the gentle craft? Prince am I none,
yet am I nobly born, as being the sole son of a shoemaker.
— Thomas Dekker, *The Shoemaker's Holiday*, 1599

IN ELIZABETHAN ENGLAND, EVERY MAN HAD HIS PLACE. William Harrison describes the social order this way: The first rank are "gentlemen of the great sort, or (as our common usage of speech is), lords and noblemen; and next unto them be knights, esquires and last of all they that are simply called gentlemen." Beneath them are "citizens and burgesses . . . , who be those that are free within the cities, and are of some substance to bear office in the same. . . . In this place also are our merchants to be installed, as amongst the citizens (although they often change estate with gentlemen, as gentlemen do with them, by a mutual conversion of the one into the other)." Far lower in rank are day laborers, servants, "and all artificers, as tailors, shoemakers, carpenters, brickmakers, masons, etc." These have "neither voice nor authority in the commonwealth, but are to be ruled and not to rule other; yet they are not altogether

Opposite: A carpenter in his workshop, planing (smoothing) a piece of wood

33

neglected, for in cities and corporate towns . . . [the authorities] make up their inquests [juries] of such manner of people."

Harrison speaks of merchants becoming gentlemen and gentlemen becoming merchants, but most men remained in the class they were born into. Still, a combination of hard work and good luck offered the possibility of rising in wealth and, sometimes, in rank as well. Nearly every young craftsman in London had the potential to eventually reach the top position in his livery company, the official organization for workers in his trade. From there he might be chosen to participate in the government of the City. So in Thomas Dekker's play *The Shoemaker's Holiday*, a shoemaker encourages his fellow craftsmen, "Ply your work today . . . ; to it pell-mell, that we may live to be lord mayors, or aldermen at least."

COMPANY LIFE

The livery companies played a major role in many aspects of life in Elizabethan London. For one thing, about three-fourths of men belonged to them. Almost every craft and trade had a company to oversee it, and it was difficult or almost impossible to work in any of these occupations without being a member of the proper company. The Worshipful Company of Carpenters, for example, required nonmembers to buy a license whenever they did any building work—otherwise they would have to pay a fine, and whatever they built might be torn down. The companies also controlled training, career advancement, manufacturing standards, and prices. In addition, they looked after their members' interests in various ways, from lobbying Parliament to pass legislation in their favor to providing housing for needy craftsmen's widows.

You could join a livery company in a few different ways. The most common way was to learn the craft or trade by serving another member as an apprentice (for more on apprenticeship, see chapter 5). If you were the son of a full member of the company, you were automatically admitted to the same company. Or, under the right circumstances, you might be allowed to join by being nominated by other members and then paying a fee.

In the normal course of advancement, once you successfully completed your apprenticeship, you were made "free of the company." Now you could work as a journeyman, a paid employee of another craftsman or tradesman. If you wanted to, you could remain a journeyman the rest of your working life. But if you were more ambitious and had the means to do so, you could set up your own shop. At this point you would become a freeman of London; this (and only this) gave you the right to buy property in the City and the right to vote in elections for aldermen. If you were successful in your business, the leaders of your company would eventually make you a liveryman, a full member. You were now allowed to wear livery: fur-lined robes and a silk hood in the distinctive colors and design of your company.

The next step up—which could take another ten years to reach— was to become a member of your company's Court of Assistants. This gave you the right to be known as a merchant. There were two classes of merchants, and their numbers were few: roughly 75 to 150 lesser merchants and only one or two dozen great merchants. If you reached this elite status (and you had to be quite wealthy to do so), you might be chosen as master of your company. The Court of Assistants, led by the master, was the company's governing body. It set punishments (usually fines) for poor workmanship, revealing craft secrets, and other breaches of company rules. It also judged disputes between members and between apprentices and their masters. The court and other company officers held their meetings in the company's hall, which was also where members assembled for feasts, elections, and other gatherings. Some of the company halls are still standing, and we can see that they all must have been handsome buildings, of which the members were very proud.

WORKING IN OTHER CITIES London was not the only city whose craftsmen and tradesmen were organized into companies (often known elsewhere as guilds), but it's the one we know most about. And we need to remember that there were regional variations in the types of work men did. Every town would likely have shoemakers, bakers, carpenters, blacksmiths, grocers, innkeepers, barbers, and so on. But only London, Oxford, and Cambridge would have a company of stationers—that is, printers and publishers. In areas where many sheep were raised, a large proportion of workers would be involved in the wool trade; cities near mines would have more industry focused on processing metals or coal. Small cities might not have very many goldsmiths or other craftsmen producing luxury items.

In coastal and port cities, of course, numerous men had jobs relating to the sea. There would be boatbuilders, providers of ships' supplies, workers to maintain harbor facilities, laborers to load and unload ships, clerks and other staff in warehouses, customs officials, and others. And of course there would be those who made their living out on the water, the sailors and fishermen. Their occupations were hard and uncomfortable, but sometimes brought great rewards.

Elizabethan England's most extraordinary seaman was Francis Drake, who rose from common sailor to naval hero. After his around-the-world voyage, Queen Elizabeth welcomed him to her court and made him a knight. He continued to sail, fighting England's enemy Spain on the seas. He raided Spanish harbors and helped defeat the Armada, the great fleet that attempted to invade England in 1588. In between voyages and battles, his activities included urban politics: he became mayor of Plymouth and then represented the city in Parliament.

GENTLEMANLY PROFESSIONS

A gentleman was a man who did not have to work with his hands or do physical labor to support himself. Traditionally he was a landowner who lived off the income from his estates. During the sixteenth century, a gentleman might also be someone who practiced a profession—so long as it was one that required him to use his mind more than his hands. This is why some merchants could be considered gentlemen: they did not personally sell goods but made financial and other arrangements for sales and purchases, imports and exports. They were wealthy investors and businessmen, far above the ranks of ordinary tradesmen.

Many gentlemen held posts at court and in the government. Foremost of these was Queen Elizabeth's most trusted councillor, William Cecil, whom she eventually raised to the nobility. Noblemen, too, filled government offices. Such positions were open only to the upper classes not just because of traditional ideas about rank but because public servants were expected to spend much of their own money in the course of fulfilling their duties. At the highest levels of government, men might receive gifts and favors from the queen, but they did not receive a salary.

Gentlemen and noblemen—who made up only 2 percent of Elizabethan England's population—were also the people with the best access to higher education. The main careers for educated men were

Sir Walter Raleigh: gentleman, knight, poet, seaman, soldier, explorer, and patron of the arts and sciences. For many years he was one of Elizabeth's favorite courtiers and captain of her personal guard. But after his secret marriage to one of Elizabeth's young ladies-in-waiting was discovered, the queen had him imprisoned and then banished from London and the court.

A LAWYER AT LEISURE

Sir Francis Bacon was a lawyer, member of Parliament, government official, essay writer, and advocate for using reason, experimentation, and observation to learn about the natural world. In his 1597 essay "Of Studies," he recommends useful reading as an ideal leisure activity for gentlemen:

Studies serve for pastimes, for ornaments, and for abilities. . . . They perfect nature, and are perfected by experience. Crafty men contemn them, simple men admire them, wise men use them. . . . Read not to contradict nor to believe, but to weigh and consider. Some books are to be tasted, others to be swallowed, and some few to be chewed and digested; that is, some books are to be read only in parts; others to be read but cursorily; and some few to be read wholly, and with diligence and attention. Reading maketh a full man, conference [conversation] a ready man, and writing an exact man. And therefore, if a man write little, he had need have a great memory; if he confer little, he had need have a present wit [lively intelligence]; and if he read little, he had need have much cunning, to seem to know that [that which] he doth not. Histories make men wise; poets, witty; the mathematics, subtle; natural philosophy [science], deep; moral [philosophy], grave; logic and rhetoric, able to contend.

Above: Sir Francis Bacon, known as one of the creators of the scientific method

in medicine, the church, and, especially, the law. The amount of legal business increased throughout the sixteenth century, creating many opportunities for lawyers. Much of their work centered on property rights, inheritances, contracts, and the buying and selling of land, for the English economy was expanding. This expansion, however, benefited mainly the already well-off, and the gap between rich and poor widened. One result was more cases of debt and bankruptcy; another was an increase in criminal cases, from petty theft to highway robbery. With the courts kept so busy, judges and lawyers prospered.

Some university-educated men might successfully combine more than one profession; Thomas Campion, for example, was both a lawyer and a physician, as well as a fine poet and composer. Others might work as secretaries or teachers or private tutors—or even as playwrights, like Christopher Marlowe. His fellow playwright William Shakespeare, however, never had the opportunity to go to university. He was the son of a glove maker (who also served as a town official) and may even have worked at that trade himself for a time. When he became an actor, he joined a profession that was not considered respectable. Ironically, he and his fellow actors often had to play the parts of nobles and gentlemen, and play them convincingly. As it turned out, Shakespeare's theater company and his plays and poems won him such esteem and wealth (which he wisely invested) that when he retired to his hometown of Stratford-upon-Avon, he was able to turn his stage role into reality and live the rest of his life as a gentleman.

City Women

Was there ever any so abused, so slandered,
so railed upon, or so wickedly handled undeservedly, as are we women?
—Jane Anger, *Her Protection for Women*, 1589

THE ROLE OF WOMEN WAS ON THE MINDS OF MANY people in sixteenth-century England. Queen Elizabeth demonstrated how much women were capable of achieving, and in the upper class there were a number of intelligent, learned, and influential women. Yet law, custom, and religion continued to regard women as inferior to men in almost every way.

There were different standards of behavior and morality for men and women, too. Women were expected to be models of obedience and quiet virtue—qualities that unfortunately could lead to them being taken advantage of by men. But women who strayed from the ideal were liable to be mocked, disgraced, and punished—by their families, their community, or even the courts. In addition, literature that put down women was growing in popularity (evidence that many women were no longer content with being quiet and obedient and that the change angered some men). A few women began

Opposite: An elderly woman making lace. Many women earned money by working in their homes at various trades connected with producing cloth and clothing.

41

to reply to these attacks and to question the double standard and other injustices that women had to live with. Most Elizabethan women, however, were working too hard just to get by to have the energy for trying to change things. Or, like the gentlewoman Martha Moulsworth, they may have wished for more education or other opportunities but made the best of what life had given them:

I had my will in house, in purse, in store,
What would a woman old or young have more?

THE RESPECTABLE HOUSEWIFE

All women were expected to marry, and they did so with the knowledge that "the duty of the husband is to be lord of all"—and this was not just his duty, but his legal right. (The only women whom the law recognized as independent people were widows.) Nevertheless, to the Dutch visitor Emanuel van Meteren in 1575, England seemed "the paradise of married women." Women in England did have more freedom than women in some other parts of Europe—respectable women in Spain, for example, were seldom allowed to leave their homes.

No doubt thinking of some of the middle-class women he'd seen in London, van Meteren wrote that wives

have the free management of the house or housekeeping. . . . They go to market to buy what they like best to eat. They are well dressed, fond of taking it easy, and commonly leave the care of household matters and drudgery to their servants. They sit before their doors, decked out in fine clothes, in order to see and be seen by the passers-by. . . . All the rest of their time they employ in walking or riding, in playing at cards or otherwise, in visiting their friends and keeping company.

Probably few married women—even in the middle class—enjoyed as much leisure time as van Meteren describes. Housewives were not paid for their work, but they were still working women. Moreover, the Elizabethan ideal of marriage was one in which the spouses were friendly companions to each other, providing emotional as well as practical support. With perhaps more than a touch of humor, pamphlet writer Jane Anger described how much men relied on their wives:

In the time of their sickness we cannot be wanted [done without], & when they are in health we for them are most necessary. They are comforted by our means: they nourished by the meats [food] we mess [prepare]: their bodies freed from diseases by our cleanliness. . . . Without our care they lie in their beds as dogs in litter, & go like lousy mackerel swimming in the heat of summer. They love to go handsomely in their apparel, and rejoice in the pride thereof, yet who is the cause of it, but our carefulness, to see that every thing about them be curious [neat and carefully made].

This portrait of Sir Thomas and Lady Jane Mansel is unusual in depicting husband and wife holding hands. It seems they must have chosen this pose out of a desire to show their sincere affection for each other.

Anger went on to describe the ways in which many men took all of this attentive housewifery for granted and even made a habit of

FRIED BREAD WITH CHERRIES:
AN ELIZABETHAN RECIPE

Cookbooks were first published in England during the reign of Elizabeth, when there was a profitable market for them among middle-class housewives. Most recipes were brief and not very specific about such things as quantities and cooking times. Here is an example from a cookbook published in 1591, followed by instructions for making this tasty treat today:

> Fry white bread in butter til it be brown and so put it into a dish, then take Cherries and take out the stones and frye them where you fried the bread then put thereto Sugar, Ginger, and Sinamon, for lacke of broth, take White or Claret Wine, boyle these togither, and that doon, serve them upon your Tostes.

Ingredients
4–6 slices of bread, depending on the size of the slices (a bakery bread will work best)
1 tablespoon butter
2 cups of fresh cherries with pits removed, or 1 can of cherry pie filling
1/4 cup white grape juice (omit this if you use pie filling)
1 tablespoon sugar (omit this if you use pie filling that contains sugar)
1/4 tablespoon ginger
1/2 tablespoon cinnamon

Melt the butter in a frying pan on medium heat, then put the bread in and cook each side until it is browned. Take out the bread and put it on plates. Put the cherries in the pan; add a bit more butter if necessary to keep them from sticking. Cook for about five minutes, stirring frequently. Add the grape juice, sugar, ginger, and cinnamon. When the liquid boils, continue cooking until the mixture reaches the desired thickness. Let it cool just a bit, then spoon it over the fried bread and enjoy!

insulting and criticizing women. "But," she asserted, "if they shall avow that women are fools, we may safely give them the lie."

Indeed, a housewife had many responsibilities that required intelligence, good sense, knowledge, skill, and planning. Even if she had servants to do the actual housework, she decided what had to be done and made sure it was done right. She took care that her family members (including servants and apprentices) were suitably clothed and probably made at least some articles of clothing herself. She planned meals and saw that supplies of food and drink were properly stored. She managed the family budget and did the shopping (or told the servants what to buy), keeping careful account of all the money spent. Oftentimes she kept supplies of herbs and made medicinal drinks, since she would be expected to nurse sick members of the household. If her family was wealthy and prominent, she might also provide medicines and other kinds of charity to less fortunate neighbors. And if her husband was a craftsman or tradesman, she probably helped him with his work, with minding his shop, and with training his apprentices.

WORKING FOR WAGES

For hundreds of years, city women and men had worked together in home-based businesses. But in the upper middle class (as we would call it), this was beginning to change. Work and life were being divided into male and female "spheres," an idea that held far into the twentieth century. The woman's sphere was in the home, as countless sermons, pamphlets, and books explained; for example:

The office [duty] of the husband is to bring in necessaries, of the wife, well to keep them. The office of the husband is, to go abroad in matters of profit, of the wife, to tarry [stay] at home, and see all be well there. The office of the husband is, to provide money, of the wife, not wastefully to spend it. The office of the husband is, to deal, and bargain with all men, of the wife, to make or meddle with no man.

A popular sermon summed it up: "We call the wife *housewife* . . . to show that a good wife keeps her house."

Such pronouncements, however, do not necessarily reflect women's real lives. Below the upper middle class, a great many Elizabethan women worked for wages, often within the home but sometimes outside it. Among the things they could earn money at were carding wool, spinning, weaving, sewing, embroidery, and knitting (especially knitting stockings). Working with cloth and clothing was an age-old occupation for women, and there were even a few women members of the Clothmakers livery company in Elizabethan London. Other women were able to earn money doing laundry. A few were entrepreneurs: Dinghen Van Den Plasse, who immigrated to London from Flanders (today's Belgium), single-handedly started a new fashion, the starched ruff. She made a good living for herself and her family starching pleated collars and teaching others how to do so; for an extra fee, she would even share her secret recipe for starch.

As already mentioned, craftsmen's wives often worked side by side with them. Sometimes if the craftsman died, his widow would carry on with the trade. This seems to have been especially common with printers' wives. Sometimes the widow would do no more than complete books left unfinished by her husband. Other times she might stay in business on her own account, like Margaret Allde, who ran a printing press for twenty-one years after her husband's death and passed her skills on to a number of apprentices.

Women could not be physicians (who had to have university degrees, which women could not get), but they provided medical services, especially for poorer people, as midwives and herbalists. In addition, we know of two women surgeons working in London in the late sixteenth century. Some women found employment as nurses in London's orphanage and two charity hospitals. Each institution also had a female official, or matron, whose duties included supervising the nurses and making certain that the facilities and bedding were kept clean. A document from Saint Bartholomew's Hospital preserves instructions for the nurses:

A fashionable young Englishwoman wearing a pleated and starched ruff

"You shall also faithfully and charitably serve and help the poor in all their griefs and diseases, as well by keeping them sweet and clean as in giving them their meats and drinks after the most . . . comfortable manner. Also you shall use unto them good and honest talk such as may comfort and amend them." In addition, the nurses spun wool and flax thread, which would be sent out to weavers to make blankets and sheets for the patients' beds.

Most female wage earners worked as servants. This was especially true of young women; one scholar estimates that 50 percent of women (and 80 percent of men) aged twenty to twenty-four were in service. After this, they would usually marry and then work primarily in their own home. There were some older women servants, though, such as wet nurses and governesses. And to the Elizabethans, taking care of children was the most natural and most important work a woman could do.

ÆTATIS
18 : M :
ANNO
1598

5

An Urban Childhood

The joys of parents are secret, and so are their griefs and fears. . . .
Children sweeten labours, but they make misfortunes more bitter:
they increase the cares of life, but they mitigate the remembrance of death.
— Francis Bacon, *Essayes*

MOST MARRIED COUPLES WANTED TO HAVE CHILDREN, and most did. Some women went through as many as a dozen pregnancies, but it was rare for all the babies to survive. One scholar estimates that between 20 and 30 percent of children did not live to the age of ten. A good portion of these died shortly after birth, which was a dangerous process for both mothers and babies. Medical knowledge and techniques were limited, so if something went wrong, there was little anyone could do.

THE EARLY YEARS

In Elizabethan England, all babies were born at home. During labor, the mother was assisted by a midwife and surrounded by supportive women friends. If all went well and both mother and baby survived the birth, celebrating began immediately, with drinks and

Opposite: This eighteen-month-old girl, the daughter of a wealthy family, is dressed in the same elaborate style as an adult woman of her class.

49

According to an inscription on this painting, these two ladies were born on the same day, married on the same day, and gave birth on the same day. They have been portrayed propped up on pillows in bed, recovering from childbirth, each with her baby dressed in rich christening clothes.

sweet treats for everyone and presents for the midwife. For the next month, the mother rarely left her room, and her friends continued to visit and assist her. At the end of that time, she went to church to give thanks to God and, if her family could afford it, gave a feast to thank her friends.

Most babies were nursed by their mothers and stayed close by them. An upper-class family, though, might hire a wet nurse to breast-feed the baby. There might also be a nursemaid to help care for it, and she and the baby would spend most of their time in the nursery. A book written to help French immigrants learn English included a scene in which a mother visits her baby in the nursery. He is wrapped in swaddling, tight bands wound around him to keep his limbs straight, according to the usual practice of the time. The mother, full of concern and affection, speaks alternately to the nurse and the baby:

Undo his swaddling bands, give him his breakfast while I am here . . . wash him before me, have you clean water? O my little heart! God bless thee, rub the crown of his head, wash his ears . . . wash his face; lift up a little his hairs, is that not some dirt I see upon his forehead? . . . pull off his shirt, thou art pretty and fat my little darling, wash his arm-pits . . . how he spreadeth his small fingers! His thumb and little finger are flea-bitten . . . is there any fleas in your chamber? . . . put him in his cradle and rock him till he sleeps but bring him to me first that I may kiss him, God send thee good rest my little boykin.

Children were usually nursed until they were around two years old. During this time, family members (and nurses, if they had them) sang them lullabies and nursery songs. Some of the rhymes they heard are still familiar to parents and children: "Three Blind Mice," "Old Mother Hubbard," "Little Jack Horner," and others. Elizabethan babies had rattles to shake and teething toys of wood (and, in well-off families, coral). After they outgrew swaddling, they were dressed in long gowns. When they started learning to walk they might have a walker, a wooden frame on wheels. Some parents attached long sleeves or strings to their toddlers' clothes; a parent could hang on to these to help steady the child as it took its first uncertain steps.

Once a child was walking and talking, it was time to start learning how to behave properly. Fathers were urged to teach their children "to use fair and gentle speech . . . with reverence and courtesy to their elders. . . . nor let your children go whither they will, but know where they go . . . and when you hear them swear or curse, lie or fight, thou shalt sharply reprove them." Children were instructed in table manners, too; for example, "Wipe not thy mouth with thy hand, nor sleeve, but with a napkin, for, for that cause it is laid before thee. Touch not any part of the meat,

A little boy wearing a lace bonnet, pleated ruff, and long gown. Boys in Elizabethan England did not start wearing pants until they were six or seven years old.

saving that which thou wilt cut off, for thyself." And don't let your sleeves drag in the sauce! But it was all right to burp during a meal. If, however, you had to spit or blow your nose, you should turn so that no one could see. And if you passed gas when other people were around, you should "let a cough cover the sound."

SCHOOLING

During Elizabeth's reign, more of the English learned to read than ever before: overall, about 30 percent of men and 10 percent of women by 1600. Nearly all of these people belonged to the upper and middle classes. Not surprisingly, then, the craftsmen, businessmen, and tradesmen of London had a high rate of literacy—as much as 60 percent in the 1580s. Children in such families might be taught to read at home, but some would be sent to school.

Schooling started around the age of six, when boys also began to wear adult-style clothes. The first school children attended was called a petty school, which taught reading, writing, basic arithmetic, and religion. Schoolteachers were usually men, and only about a third of them had a university degree. Most of the students were boys; if girls got an education at all, they generally got it at home.

BOYS' EDUCATION   After a boy learned to read and write in the petty school, he could go on to grammar school. Only a small percentage of boys did so, however. Many had to start working, helping out in the family business, or it was time for them to begin an apprenticeship. Besides, grammar school usually cost money; most families couldn't afford the fees, and there were only a limited number of scholarships for academically gifted pupils.

Many of London's livery companies ran grammar schools; oth-

AN ARITHMETIC LESSON

During the 1500s, doing arithmetic got far easier than it had been in previous centuries. Why? Because during this time, the English switched from Roman numerals to the Hindu-Arabic numerals that we still use today. This change simplified all mathematical operations. It probably also meant that students started getting more math work. Perhaps they were assigned word problems like this one from a 1581 arithmetic manual: "There is a cat at the foot of a tree the length of 300 feet. This cat goeth upward each day 17 feet and descendeth each night 12 feet." How long would it take the cat to reach the top of the tree?*

*60 days.

ers were operated by churches or by private citizens. All schools were quite strict and expected a lot from their students. The main subjects were languages and literature: Latin and Greek, and sometimes Hebrew, French, and/or German. The works that the boys read and translated taught them history, philosophy, rhetoric (the persuasive use of language), and religion along the way, and they might also receive some instruction in science, mathematics, and music.

Like students everywhere, these boys sometimes got bored and doodled in their schoolbooks. One boy scribbled the name *Elizabeth* all over a text about Julius Caesar and wrote in the margin:

The rose is red, the leaves are green,
God save Elizabeth, our noble queen.

Since this boy expressed himself so patriotically, he may not have been punished for letting his mind wander from his lessons. Most schoolteachers, however, enforced discipline by beating reluctant

The grammar school in Stratford-upon-Avon, where Shakespeare learned Latin and literature alongside about forty other boys, ages seven to fourteen. The school was housed in a large room above the town hall. The building is still standing and in use today.

or misbehaving pupils. In some schools, boys could be beaten for speaking English instead of Latin, or even for having dirty hands or uncombed hair. It's hard to imagine, though, that anyone in grammar school had the time or energy to get into real trouble, since the school day could stretch from 5:00 AM to 7:00 PM, with lessons interrupted only for prayers and meals.

GIRLS' EDUCATION Even though England was ruled by an extremely intelligent and learned woman, girls did not have the same educational opportunities as boys. Many people believed that learning was inappropriate and even harmful for females. Others, like Juan Luis Vives, recommended that girls be educated, but only in those ways that would directly benefit their future husbands and children:

A wise woman should have in mind merry tales, and histories

. . . wherewith she may refresh her husband, and make him merry, when he is weary. And also she shall learn precepts of wisdom, to exhort him unto virtue. . . . Neither a virtuous mother ought to refuse learning on the book, but now and then study and read holy and wise men's books: and though she do it not for her own sake, at the leastwise for her children, that she may teach them and make them good.

As a practical matter, Richard Mulcaster, head of the prestigious Merchant Taylors' School in London, pointed out, "young maidens must give me leave to speak of boys first: because naturally the male is more worthy, and politically he is more employed. . . . [T]he bringing up of young maidens in any kind of learning, is but an accessory by the way."

Although some petty schools did admit girls, most grammar schools and both universities were closed to them—a fact that poet Martha Moulsworth lamented:

Two universities we have of men,
O that we had but one of women then!

Nearly all girls were taught at home by their mothers, mainly learning the skills they would need to run a household. Fathers might also share some of their knowledge—Martha Moulsworth's father saw to it that she learned Latin, although she never had any chance to use it later. Girls in wealthy families received additional education from governesses and perhaps tutors. In all but a few cases, however, lessons in music, singing, and dancing were more likely to be emphasized than such subjects as philosophy, mathematics, and languages.

A BELOVED GOVERNESS

In 1617, near the end of her life, Lady Grace Mildmay remembered some of the teaching she received from her governess, Mrs. Hamblyn: "When she did see me idly disposed, she would set me to cipher [do math] with my pen, and to cast up and prove great sums and accounts, and sometimes set me to write a supposed [pretend, for practice] letter to this or that body concerning such and such things." Mildmay recalled that Mrs. Hamblyn "proved very religious, wise, and chaste, and all good virtues that might be in a woman very constantly settled in her, for, from her youth she made good use of all things that ever she did read see or hear; and observed all companies that ever she came in, good or bad: so she could give a right censure [opinion] and true judgment of most things, and give wise counsel upon any occasion."

Above: A lady holding a small book. Nearly all upper-class women could read English, and some learned to read ancient and foreign languages, too.

PREPARING FOR ADULTHOOD

After five to ten years of grammar school, finishing usually around the age of fourteen, some boys went on to higher education. They could attend university in Oxford or Cambridge, where they studied basically the same subjects as in grammar school, but in greater depth. After a couple years at university, they might decide to study law at the Inns of Court. The Inns were in London, near the law courts just west of the City. When the courts were in session, lawyers stayed in the Inns, and so students went there to learn law from those who practiced it. There were four main Inns (all of which still exist), each with one or two subordinate Inns; a student would join only one of them. Some students stayed at their Inn just long enough to learn the basics of legal thought and procedure. To actually become a lawyer required at least seven years of diligent study.

Sir Edward Coke became a lawyer in 1578, a member of Parliament in 1589, speaker of the House of Commons in 1592, and attorney general in 1593. He wrote several books on English common law, and these remained authoritative legal references for nearly three hundred years.

Students at the Inns learned the Common Law, which was based on the body of legal decisions made in the past. This reliance on precedent was not only the cornerstone of English law but became a foundation of legal practice in England's colonies and the countries descended from them. During the Elizabethan period, though, there were few law books. Students learned mainly by observing lawyers and judges in the courts and by discussing legal points with the lawyers of the Inn. There were plenty of opportunities for this, since all members ate every meal together in the Inn's common hall. Each Inn also had a chapel, which all members were required to attend, and gardens where members could exercise and relax.

A goldsmith's workshop, with a young apprentice *(left)* operating a piece of machinery and an older one *(right)* heating metal in a furnace, while the master goldsmith and his assistants work at tasks that require greater precision and experience

The universities and Inns of Court were for a minority of boys. Most others received their advanced education through apprentice-ships—one scholar has estimated that two out of three adult male Londoners had been apprentices during their youth. The great majority of apprentices were boys, but a few crafts and trades—the glove makers, for example—did apprentice girls from time to time. Many London apprentices were not native to the city; 40 percent of the apprentices in the Fishmongers livery company, for instance, were from Scotland. Boys did not have to follow in their fathers' footsteps; although a father normally decided whom his son would apprentice with, he tried to choose a trade that would suit the boy.

Apprenticeship lasted at least seven years, and at least till the apprentice was twenty-four years old. During that time he lived with his master, who was required to give him food, shelter, clothing, and training. In return, he assisted the master at his work and helped out around the house, even with such humble tasks as carrying water

The City

from the river. The apprentice was expected to be absolutely obedient to his master; if he wasn't, the master had the right to whip him. On the other hand, if a master beat an apprentice without reason or otherwise mistreated him, he could be punished by his livery company or guild, with a fine or even imprisonment.

When a young man completed his apprenticeship, his master often gave him a gift of tools or money so that he could set up his own workshop and household. The new craftsman might also take out a loan, either from his former master or his company, to help get his business started. Then, once he could afford to support a family, he could get married. By that time he would probably be in his late twenties, and his bride would be only a few years younger. She, too, had to be both socially and financially ready to marry, and may have spent as many as ten years working as a servant, earning money for her dowry and practicing the household skills she'd need once she had a husband and children.

Rest and Recreation

I think it not evil that sometimes a Christian man play and refresh himself.
— THOMAS WILCOX, *A GLASSE FOR GAMESTERS*, 1581

MARRIAGE, THE BIRTH OF A HEALTHY BABY, A BOY'S FIRST day of wearing breeches—occasions like these were times to take a break from work and celebrate with friends and family. So, too, were holidays. Religious holidays were observed with church services, and usually with feasting and other festivities as well. Many city dwellers also continued to celebrate old folk holidays such as May Day, when people would leave the city to "walk into the sweet meadows and green woods, there to rejoice their spirits with the harmony of birds." Then, according to London tailor and historian John Stow, there would be May games and dancing around maypoles, all with great merriment.

One of the greatest occasions for a city was a visit by the queen. Londoners of course had many opportunities to catch a glimpse of her, hear her speak, and enjoy the pageantry that surrounded her. But Elizabeth did not confine herself to London. Always mindful of the

Opposite: In a scene painted around the time of Elizabeth's childhood, a young man with his hat pulled down over his eyes plays blind man's buff with two ladies in a rose garden. Such games were enjoyed by children and adults alike.

61

importance of staying connected to her people, she spent most summers of her reign visiting different parts of England.

When plans for a royal visit were announced, cities looked forward both to the honor of the monarch's presence and to the increase in business it would bring, and they launched into preparations. The mayor and aldermen would order streets cleared and widened, public bathrooms cleaned, pigs and cows kept out of the roads. Citizens put fresh plaster on their house fronts, hung out tapestries or painted cloths, and decorated doors and windows with garlands. City musicians got new uniforms and rehearsed the music they would play for the queen; children practiced poems they would recite and dances they would perform; aldermen's wives prepared special foods to serve her.

When the great day finally came and the queen arrived, no one was disappointed. Elizabeth truly appreciated everything townsfolk did in her honor, from mayors' speeches to little girls' demonstrations of their weaving and knitting. And the people were impressed not only by her magnificence but by the kind and gracious way she welcomed anyone to come up and speak to her:

> Private persons and magistrates, country people and children came joyfully and without any fear to wait upon her. Her ears were then open to the complaints of the afflicted, and of those that had been in any way injured. . . . She was never angry with the uncourtly approach. . . . Nor was there anything in the whole course of her reign that more won the hearts of the people.

PLEASANT PASTIMES

On days when nothing special was happening, townspeople with some leisure could find many ways to pass the time at home. Music

was one of them—so long as you (or someone among your friends and family) were able to sing or play an instrument, since there was no such thing as recorded music in any form. Then there were games: card games, chess, backgammon, games with spinning tops, games with dice, games like jacks—something for everyone. A major pastime was reading, now that so many people were literate. Those who couldn't read could listen to others—in fact, almost everyone enjoyed being read to, so often one family member would read aloud while others worked at sewing, spinning, knitting, or mending tools.

When you didn't want a quiet afternoon or evening at home, the cities, especially London, offered many public places of recreation. You could go to the fields outside town to ride, stroll, wrestle, or practice archery. You might be able to take a walk in the gardens of the Inns of Court or the livery companies' meeting halls. Some

This 1879 painting by Walter Duncan illustrates a line from Shakespeare's play *Twelfth Night*: "If music be the food of love, play on."

company halls had bowling alleys, for lawn bowling. There were places where you could watch tightrope walkers, and fencers exhibiting their skill in swordplay. Or you could just go to one of the "many inns, taverns and beer-gardens scattered about the city, where much amusement may be had with eating, drinking, fiddling and the rest."

There was music everywhere. "All Cities, Towns, and villages swarm with companies of musicians and fiddlers," commented one Elizabethan traveler. More than seventy towns had municipal bands called waits. In smaller cities the waits might be only three or four musicians; the London waits had twelve, and about twenty apprentices. The waits performed on official occasions, at mayors' dinners, at festivals, and so on. In many places they were supposed to play every morning and evening. During spring and summer, the London waits gave free concerts from the balcony of the Royal Exchange every Sunday, "to the great contentment of all who hear."

As odd as it may seem to us, many of the same Elizabethans who loved music and poetry also enjoyed some very bloody spectacles. On the south bank of the Thames, there were rings for bull baiting and bear baiting. *Baiting* meant that the animal was tethered to a stake and then attacked by dogs. It was a ferocious and bloody entertainment, yet there were crowds of people who agreed with Shakespeare's character Abraham Slender in *The Merry Wives of Windsor*: "Be there bears i'th' town? . . . I love the sport well."

The Play's the Thing

London's southern suburbs were home not just to the bull and bear rings but to the strong-smelling industries of tanning, soap making, and felt making. Here, too, were such unrespectable places as prisons, poorhouses, alehouses—and theaters, including the most renowned of all, the Globe. Built in 1599, the Globe was owned by the Lord Chamberlain's Men, whose previous home had been the Theatre, in one of the northern suburbs. (As the company's name indicates, there were no women among the actors. During this period in England, women's roles were played by boys.) One of the leading members of the Lord Chamberlain's Men was William Shakespeare. In the first year of the Globe's operation, it saw the performance of two new Shakespeare plays, *Henry V* and *Julius Caesar.* That same year he also began work on *As You Like It* and *Hamlet.* By this time he had written about twenty plays, most of which his company was still performing, along with works by Ben Jonson and other playwrights.

The Globe, with a flag flying to advertise that a play would be performed that afternoon. As part owner of the theater, Shakespeare probably oversaw much of its construction.

Plays were an important part of life for many Londoners—one scholar estimates that probably one-third of the adult population went to the theater at least once a month. Some, like the arts-loving Earl of Southampton, went five or six times a week. Plays were staged almost every afternoon, and never the same play two days in a row. The theaters had little in the way of sets and props, but costumes were gorgeous and elaborate. To protect these costumes—and the actors wearing them—from the elements, there was a canopy over the stage. There was a covered gallery, too, for people who paid a higher admission fee, and if they paid just a bit more, they also got a cushioned seat in a special section. But most of the audience stood on the ground in front of the stage (which was five feet high, so that everyone could see); for this reason they were called groundlings.

Playwrights offered something for almost everyone. Christopher Marlowe specialized in violent historical epics and thundering dramas, such as *Tamburlaine*, about a cruel conqueror, and *Doctor Faustus*, about a scholar who makes a deal with the devil. Thomas Dekker was particularly successful with his plays about London's middle class. Ben Jonson was just starting his career in the 1590s, during which he wrote mainly satirical comedies. Shakespeare, however, was the playwright who offered audiences the widest range: comedy, history, tragedy, action, romance, fantasy—sometimes all in the same play. People were moved to laughter, tears, and delight during the performances, and left the theaters with Shakespeare's vivid characters and wonderful words imprinted in their memories. Poet Leonard Digges observed this himself after a performance of *Julius Caesar*: "O, how the audience / Were ravished! With what wonder they went thence!"

Some Londoners, however, did not like the theater at all. Among

The Drama of Life

In *Hamlet*, Shakespeare wrote that the purpose of plays was "to hold as 'twere the mirror up to nature." In the following passage from *As You Like It*, he speaks of life itself as being a kind of play.

All the world's a stage,
And all the men and women merely players.
They have their exits and their entrances,
And one man in his time plays many parts,
His acts being seven ages. At first the infant,
Mewling and puking in the nurse's arms.
Then the whining schoolboy with his satchel
And shining morning face, creeping like snail
Unwillingly to school. And then the lover,
Sighing like furnace, with a woeful ballad
Made to his mistress' eyebrow. Then, a soldier,
Full of strange oaths, and bearded like the pard,*   *leopard
Jealous in honour, sudden, and quick in quarrel,
Seeking the bubble reputation
Even in the cannon's mouth. And then the justice,* *justice of the peace
In fair round belly with good capon lined,
With eyes severe and beard of formal cut,
Full of wise saws* and modern instances;** *sayings **examples
And so he plays his part. The sixth age shifts
Into the lean and slippered pantaloon,*   *foolish old man
With spectacles on nose and pouch on side,
His youthful hose, well saved, a world too wide
For his shrunk shank, and his big, manly voice,
Turning again toward childish treble, pipes
And whistles in his sound. Last scene of all,
That ends this strange, eventful history,
Is second childishness and mere oblivion,
Sans* teeth, sans eyes, sans taste, sans everything. *without

them were, very often, the aldermen and the Lord Mayor, who repeatedly petitioned the Privy Council to close down the theaters. They complained that plays contained "nothing but profane fables, lascivious matters, cozening devices, and scurrilous behaviors"—that is, they were indecent, immoral, and full of trickery—and that audiences were full of "idle and dangerous persons." But the Privy Council almost always took the side of the theaters: "for honest recreation sake, in respect that her Majesty sometimes took delight in those pastimes, it had been thought not unfit . . . to allow of certain companies of players in London, partly that they might thereby attain more dexterity and perfection in that profession, the better to content her Majesty." In other words, the queen liked plays, so the theaters stayed open.

From time to time, the acting companies went on tour; otherwise people outside London had little opportunity to see professional plays. Instead, townsfolk might satisfy their taste for drama by attending sessions of the local law court. Trials were popular spectacles, as poet Michael Drayton described:

Like some great learned judge, to end a weighty cause,
Well furnished with the force of arguments and laws, . . .
And at the point to give the last and final doom
The people crowding near within the pester'd room.
A slow soft murmuring moves amongst the wond'ring throng,
As though with open ears they would devour his tongue.

The "doom," or judgment, might also be a source of entertainment. Many punishments were carried out in public: convicted offenders could be put into the stocks, driven through the streets in a cart, or tied onto a horse backward wearing a sign on which their crime was described. More seriously, they might be flogged at a public whipping post or forced to walk through town with a constable following and whipping them. Execution was the fate of the worst offenders—murderers, traitors, highway robbers, and so on—and hangings attracted large crowds. For many people the spectacles of punishment gave them not only a break from their everyday routines but also a sense of reassurance: first, that order was being maintained and second, that perhaps their own problems were not so bad after all.

Surviving in the City

The plague full swift goes by;
I am sick, I must die.
Lord, have mercy on us!
— THOMAS NASHE, "A LITANY IN TIME OF PLAGUE," 1592

ONE OF THE HARDEST THINGS TO CAPTURE ABOUT THE PAST is its sounds. Elizabethan London must have been full of noise from the cries of street vendors, the traffic, and the range of everyday activities. Playwright Thomas Dekker described the constant commotion this way:

> In every street, carts and coaches make such a thundering as if the world ran upon wheels; at every corner, men, women, and children meet in such shoals, that posts are set up of purpose to strengthen the houses, lest with jostling one another they should shoulder them down. Besides, hammers are beating in one place, tubs hooping in another, pots clinking in a third, water-tankards [water-carts] running at tilt in a fourth. Here are porters sweating under burdens, there

Opposite: Life was difficult, and dangerous, for many in England's over-populated, overbuilt capital city. Municipal authorities were hard-pressed to keep London safe and clean.

71

merchants' men bearing bags of money. Chapmen (as if they were at leap-frog) skip out of one shop into another. Tradesmen (as if they were dancing galliards) are lusty at legs and never stand still.

The image of "shoals" of people jostling one another in this selection reminds us how crowded many Elizabethan cities were. And London was growing so rapidly that the situation was particularly severe. It's estimated that about 4,000 young men came to London from other parts of Great Britain every year to begin apprenticeships, and about 750 to study in the Inns of Court. Then there were all the thousands of country people who migrated to the city in search of work. Refugees from war and religious persecution in other parts of Europe, especially France and the Low Countries, added still more thousands to London's population. Life was already very hard for many city dwellers; the uncontrolled growth only increased the challenge of survival.

HAZARDOUS CONDITIONS

As more people crammed into London, the cityscape changed dramatically. John Stow described an area near one of the City gates where during his youth there had been "pleasant fields, very commodious for citizens therein to walk, shoot, and otherwise to recreate and refresh their dull spirits in the sweet and wholesome air." But by the time he wrote his *Survey of London* (published in 1598), this same area was "a continual building throughout," packed with tenements, workshops, and garbage piles.

Urban crowding created a variety of difficulties and hazards. For one thing, it made fire an ever-present danger—all those wooden buildings so close together, and within them fire was in constant use for light, heat, cooking, and various manufacturing processes. Moreover, there were no organized firefighting services, so a stray spark or a knocked-over candle could have disastrous consequences. Shakespeare's hometown, for example, was ravaged by fires two years in a row in the 1590s.

With waste in the streets and so many people with limited access to bathwater, Elizabethan cities probably stank much of the time. For this reason the well-to-do often hung from their belt a pomander, a silver ball pierced with small holes and filled with rose petals, cloves, cinnamon, or other fragrant substances—the wearer could sniff the pomander whenever unpleasant odors became overpowering. Alternatively, people held small bouquets of herbs and flowers under their noses or stuck cloves in their nostrils. Smells were a problem indoors, too, so a careful housewife might scent her home with the fragrant steam from a boiling pot of rosemary, marjoram, bay leaves, cloves, vinegar, and rosewater. Such measures were doubly important to the Elizabethans because it was widely believed that some diseases were caused by bad smells.

One of the worst effects of crowding was the ease with which sickness could spread. Typhoid, caused by drinking filthy water, struck again and again. Marshy areas around the Thames bred malaria-carrying mosquitoes. Smallpox was an almost constant presence, killing many and leaving numerous survivors scarred or even blind. Tuberculosis was another serious disease that occurred in high numbers—in one London neighborhood, it was responsible for a quarter of all deaths in a seventeen-year period.

The most dreaded disease of all, however, was bubonic plague. There were isolated cases each summer, larger outbreaks every few years, and major epidemics at least three times during Elizabeth's reign. One of these plague epidemics killed more than 10,000

In this humorous illustration, the artist has imagined Sir Walter Raleigh, clay pipe in hand, reacting to his first experience of smoking tobacco.

Londoners, and each of the others took the lives of around 25,000. So when plague struck, panic set in. People with the horribly contagious disease were quarantined, shut into their houses for twenty days or more; no one, including uninfected family members, could leave or enter (but at least the neighborhood church paid someone, usually an impoverished old woman, to take food to the house every day—and notify the authorities when there was a death). In bad plague years, all public gatherings, except church services, were banned. Places of amusement, including the theaters, were shut down, leaving actors and others unemployed for an indefinite period. Anyone who could afford to leave the city fled to the countryside in hope of finding healthier air. That was the only hope of safety, for as one Elizabethan author wrote, "What disease is there in the world so venomous in infecting, so full of pain in suffering, so hasty in devouring, and so difficult in curing, as the plague is?"

Another author, though, believed a cure for the plague—and many other ailments—had been found: tobacco. He wrote, "Our age has discovered nothing from the New World which will be numbered among the remedies more valuable and efficacious than this plant for sores, wounds, affections of the throat and chest, and the fever of the plague." Most Elizabethans agreed that tobacco was a supreme medicine, and many got into the habit of pipe smoking.

Very few suspected that they had simply found a new way to endanger their health, although there were those who believed smoking was a sinful indulgence. As Swiss traveler Thomas Platter observed, Englishmen used tobacco "so abundantly that their preachers cry out on them for their self-destruction and I am told the inside of one man's veins after death was found to be covered in soot just like a chimney." A character in one of Ben Jonson's plays agreed: "This roguish tobacco . . . [is] good for nothing but to choke a man, and fill him full of smoke and embers."

A SPIRIT OF PUBLIC SERVICE

Of the thousands of people who came to London every year in search of a better life, many met with bitter disappointment. They encountered overcrowding, rats, garbage, stinking gutters and drainage ditches, rampant disease. They might not be able to find a decent job or affordable housing. Immigrants were often treated with suspicion, and hostility toward foreigners sometimes erupted into riots. Many residents of London fell into poverty. Some turned to begging, others to crime. Still more—as much as 15 percent of the population—depended completely or partly on charity in order to get by.

Everyone in London recognized the problems. The national government tried to handle them by passing "poor laws." These required the unimpoverished residents of each parish, or neighborhood, to give money to their local church, which would then use the collected funds to help the parish poor. In general, only people who could not work due to age, illness, injury, or disability were allowed to receive this assistance. All able-bodied people were expected to work; those who turned to begging instead could be whipped through the streets or sent to a "house of correction," where they were made to labor at spinning, grinding grain, and sim-

One way to punish troublemakers was simply to cast them out beyond the city gates.

ilar tasks. When people were both willing and able to work, but still could not manage to support themselves, the parish was supposed to find them a suitable job.

Unfortunately, there were too many needy people for parish-based assistance to help them all, especially in London. In 1582, a writer named John Howe asked,

> Why do the streets yet swarm with beggars, that no man can stand or stay in any church or street but presently 10 or 12 beggars come breathing in his face, many of them having their plague sores and other contagious diseases running on them? . . . What is the cause that so many little pretty children, boys and girls, do wander up and down the streets . . . and lie under hedges and stalls in the night?

Such sights moved many of the wealthy to do what they could

to relieve the suffering of the poor. Rich people (usually men, because women rarely had control of large sums of money) founded and donated to almshouses, contributed to the city-run hospitals that took care of orphans and the sick poor, helped penniless girls with their dowries and young craftsmen with getting a start in business. Such good works continued even after death. It was common for well-to-do men to leave money to charity in their wills, sometimes making very specific bequests. One merchant, for example, earmarked a sum of money to buy pails for sixty poor women so that they could support themselves as water carriers.

Many London merchants, craftsmen, and tradesmen left substantial sums to their livery companies to use for charitable purposes. The companies may well have been the most active institutions in the fight against poverty. First, they took care of their own members, providing assistance if illness or injury kept them from working. If a member died and left a widow and children with no means of support, the company helped them, too. Livery companies established and ran schools and almshouses, gave scholarships to poor boys to go to grammar school or university, arranged for poor people to receive free food and clothing, and so on. Many of the companies' charitable activities benefited not just members but other people in need, too. True, the companies and their members couldn't help everyone—but they had a spirit of public service and a sense of belonging to a larger community, in which it was just as important to do good works as to do good work. Like the worthy London goldsmith in one of Ben Jonson's plays, they could claim with pride,

The gain of honest pains is never base:
From trades, from arts, from valor, honor springs.

GLOSSARY

alderman a member of a city council

almshouse a home for the poor

apprentice a young person being trained in a craft or trade by assisting and working for a master in that craft or trade

chapman a merchant or tradesman

conduit a channel constructed to carry water from its main source

courtier a person who lived at or regularly attended a ruler's court

dowry money, property, and goods that a bride brought into her marriage

galliard a lively dance

journeyman from the French word *journée*, "a day's work"; a craftsman who had completed apprenticeship but was employed by another craftsman rather than in his own workshop

livery company a London organization of craftsmen or tradesmen; *livery* refers to the special clothing that marked people as members of the company. In London and other cities there were also companies that did not have livery (a special privilege), but functioned the same way. The term *guild* is often used instead of *company*.

Low Countries today's Netherlands and Belgium. During Elizabeth's time they were ruled by Spain.

militia a locally based armed force made up regular citizens (as opposed to professional soldiers). In Elizabethan England, all able-bodied males sixteen to sixty might be required to serve in the militias in a national emergency.

Parliament the legislative branch of the English government, made up of the House of Commons and the House of Lords. In Elizabeth's time, it only met when the monarch summoned it, and its main function was to approve taxes and major changes in policy.

Privy Council the queen's closest advisers, who ran government departments and saw that her decisions were put into effect

rhetoric the art of using language to persuade through eloquent speech or writing

tenement rental property. Elizabethan tenements were often rows of small houses, each house sharing side walls with its neighbors.

For Further Reading

Ashby, Ruth. *Elizabethan England.* New York: Benchmark Books, 1999.

Ferris, Julie. *Shakespeare's London: A Guide to Elizabethan London.* New York: Kingfisher, 2000.

Greenblatt, Miriam. *Elizabeth I and Tudor England.* New York: Benchmark Books, 2002.

Hinds, Kathryn. *Life in the Renaissance: The City.* New York: Benchmark Books, 2004.

Langley, Andrew. *Shakespeare's Theatre.* New York: Oxford University Press, 1999.

Rosen, Michael. *Shakespeare: His Work and His World.* Cambridge, MA: Candlewick Press, 2001.

Yancey, Diane. *Life in the Elizabethan Theater.* San Diego: Lucent Books, 1997.

Online Information

Best, Michael. *Shakespeare's Life and Times.*
http://ise.uvic.ca/Library/SLT/intro/introsubj.html

The Map of Early Modern London.
http://mapoflondon.uvic.ca/map.php

Renaissance: The Elizabethan World.
http://elizabethan.org

Selected Bibliography

Greenblatt, Stephen. *Will in the World: How Shakespeare Became Shakespeare.* New York: W. W. Norton, 2004.

Hentzner, Paul. *Itinerarium Angliae (1612), with a translation by Robert Bentley, and annotations by Horace Walpole.* Hypertext edition by Dana F. Sutton, 2004. http://www.philological.bham.ac.uk/hentzner

Orlin, Lena Cowen. *Elizabethan Households: An Anthology.* Washington, DC: The Folger Shakespeare Library, 1995.

Picard, Liza. *Elizabeth's London: Everyday Life in Elizabethan London.* New York: St. Martin's Press, 2003.

Pritchard, R. E., ed. *Shakespeare's England: Life in Elizabethan and Jacobean Times.* Stroud, Gloucestershire: Sutton Publishing, 1999.

Rowse, A. L. *The England of Elizabeth: The Structure of Society.* Madison: University of Wisconsin Press, 1978.

Shapiro, James. *A Year in the Life of William Shakespeare: 1599.* New York: HarperCollins, 2005.

Walker, Kim. *Women Writers of the English Renaissance.* New York: Twayne Publishers, 1996.

Weir, Alison. *The Life of Elizabeth I.* New York: Ballantine Books, 1998.

INDEX

Page numbers for illustrations are in boldface